ideas number 27

D1210898

Contents

Edited by Wayne Rice; Drawings by Dan Pegoda

Your Idea May Be Worth $100

It's worth at least $10.00 if we publish it in a future volume of **Ideas**. And it's worth $100.00 if it is chosen as the outstanding idea of the book it appears in.

It's not really a contest. It's just our way of saying "thanks" for sharing your creativity with us. If you have a good idea that worked well with your group, send it in. We'll look it over and decide whether or not we can include it in a future **Ideas** book. If we do, we'll send you at least ten bucks!

In addition to that, our **Ideas** editors will select one especially creative idea from each new book as the outstanding idea of that particular book. To its contributor, we'll send a check for $100.00

So don't let your good ideas go to waste. Write them down and send them to us along with this card. When you do, try to explain your ideas as completely as you can (without getting ridicu-lous), and include any sample materials, illustra-tions, diagrams, or photos that might be helpful.

FILL OUT BELOW

Name _____

Address _____ State_____ Zip _____

City _____

I hereby submit the attached idea(s) to Youth Specialties for publication in IDEAS, and guarantee that to my knowledge the publication of these ideas by Youth Specialties does not violate any copyright belonging to another party. I also understand that I will receive payment for these ideas, the exact amount to be determined by Youth Specialties, pay-able on publication in IDEAS.

Signature _____

Write or type out your idea(s) and attach to this form or a copy of this form. Put your name somewhere on the idea(s) as well. Mail to Youth Specialties, 1224 Greenfield Drive, El Cajon, CA 92021. Ideas submitted to Youth Specialties can-not be returned.

How to use this book.

We're leaving it entirely up to you.

Inside are dozens of ideas that you can use anytime, anywhere, and anyway you want.

You decide for yourself.

Use the ideas that best fit your particular personality, locale, youth group size, age group and situation.

And don't be afraid to try something new once in a while.

But on the other hand, don't feel you have to use an idea just because it's there.

Allow this book to spark your own creativity.

Remember that any idea can be improved by changing it, adding to it, combining it with another, or only using part of it.

After all, that's what this book is for:

To help you design a youth program that will best meet the needs of your kids.

We can't do it for you.

But we can help.

HOW TO GET MORE IDEAS

There are many other outstanding books like this one in the complete IDEAS library, each with a different assortment of great youth programming ideas. Since 1968, Youth Specialties has collected more than three thousand tried and tested ideas from America's most creative youth workers and has published them in IDEAS, with several new books being published each year.

All 31 volumes of ideas are still available from Youth Specialties by using the order form below. Each book is different and contains dozens of ideas that you can use right now. The first twenty volumes have been updated and re-published as five "Combo" books, with four volumes in each book. These books are $17.95 each and are a real bargain. The other books (volumes 21 through 31) are available at the single volume price of $6.95 each. The entire IDEAS library may be purchased for a total of $140.00, a savings of over $26.00.

HOW TO KEEP IDEAS COMING

A new volume (52 pages) of IDEAS is published every quarter (four per year) and you may automatically receive each of the next four books by ordering a subscription to IDEAS for $24.95. It's the best way to make sure you always have plenty of the latest youth programming ideas available anywhere. To start your subscription to IDEAS, use the order form below.

IDEAS ORDER FORM

Check desired books below: *Single volumes of Ideas at $6.95 each:*

☐ Ideas 1-4 ($17.95)   ☐ Ideas 13-16 ($17.95)   ☐ Ideas #21   ☐ Ideas #25
☐ Ideas 5-8 ($17.95)   ☐ Ideas 17-20 ($17.95)   ☐ Ideas #22   ☐ Ideas #26
☐ Ideas 9-12 ($17.95)   ☐ Ideas #23   ☐ Ideas #27
                                                       ☐ Ideas #24   ☐ Ideas #28

☐ Entire Ideas Library *(31 volumes for $140.00)*   ☐ Ideas #29

☐ Subscription to Ideas *(four volumes for $24.95)*   ☐ Ideas #30

☐ New Ideas Index *($7.95)*   ☐ Ideas #31

Check method of payment below:

☐ Check or money order enclosed. *(We pay shipping. California residents add 6% sales tax.)*

☐ Please Bill Me. *(Shipping charges plus a 5% billing charge will be added to the total amount.)*

Name _____

Address _____

City_____ State_____ Zip code _____

Church or Organization _____

Have you ever ordered from Youth Specialties before?   ☐ Yes   ☐ No

Clip and mail to: Youth Specialties, 1224 Greenfield Dr., El Cajon, CA 92021

Chapter One

Crowd Breakers

ABDUL THE MAGNIFICENT

This is a mind reading stunt which, when done right, is downright spooky. Give each person a slip of paper and ask them to write a short sentence on it. The slips are then folded, collected, and "Abdul" (who can be dressed appropriately) proceeds to perform the task of reading the sentences to the group without opening the papers.

How is it done? Abdul also puts one slip of paper in the box along with the others, only he puts some kind of identifying mark on his. When the reading starts, he picks one of the slips from the box, rubs it on his forehead without opening it, and offers any sentence as a guess as to what is on the paper. He then looks at the paper, and to his dismay he is wrong, but that will soon be forgotten. He can blame it on the fact that the "spirits" aren't quite right yet, but that the next one should be better. It's important not to dwell on this mistake long. Just get on with the next one. It's also important not to reveal what was actually on the paper guessed incorrectly. Just get rid of it and go on. Another slip of paper is held to the forehead, and Abdul then repeats the sentence which was actually on the previous paper. After rubbing his forehead, he opens this second slip of paper, confirms that he is correct, and asks the person who wrote that sentence to identify it. Everyone is impressed. Another paper is drawn and again, Abdul repeats the sentence that was on the previously opened slip. Each time he opens up a slip of paper to see if he is "correct", he is actually learning the next sentence. The important thing is to stay one slip ahead. When he comes to his own slip, which has been held until last, he repeats the sentence on the previous slip, and that takes care of all of them. If this is done smoothly, it will really baffle the group. (Contributed by Mike Andujar, Los Gatos, California)

COMMON GROUND

This is a small group experience that is fun and that helps kids to get to know each other a lot better. The group is divided up into discussion groups of from five to seven per group, and then each group is given a sheet of instructions. The basic idea is for each group to come up with something that they *all* like or *all* dislike in a variety of categories (see list below). They are encouraged to be honest rather than just trying to "go for the points."

For each consensus reached, the group will receive a certain number of points (whatever you want). You could give ten points for any answer that everyone in the group had in common, and fewer points for answers that only some of the kids in the group had in common. For example, if only five out of the group of seven had a particular thing in common, then they would only get five points instead of the ten. Set a time limit of around ten minutes for this exercise.

Category	Like	Dislike
1. Food 2. Game 3. TV Show 4. Gift received 5. School subject 6. Chore at home 7. Song 8. Hobby 9. Way to spend Saturday 10. Sport		

Next, the group is to come up with as many other shared experiences as they possibly can. They would receive additional points for each one of these. For example:

1. Got a B on last report card
2. Been sad over the death of a loved one
3. Been stood up by a friend
4. Went on a back-packing trip

Give the group five minutes to try and come up with as many of these common experiences as possible. Any experience is acceptable, so long as each person in the group has shared that experience. Someone in the group should act as secretary and write them down as they are named by the group and agreed to. At the end of the time limit, the group can total up its points.

This exercise is excellent for "breaking the ice" and helps kids to see just how much they have in common with each other. (Contributed by Syd Schnaars, Delaware, Ohio)

COMMUNITY QUIZ

This is a crowd breaker that works great as a mixer. It works best in situations when you know everyone who will be in attendance. You will need to contact each person in advance, get certain information from them, and then include that information in a written quiz that you print up before your meeting or event. The quiz should contain the same number of multiple choice or true-false questions as there are people (or you could have more than one question for each person).

You can then use the quiz in one of several ways. One way is to simply give everyone a copy of the quiz and they begin milling around the room asking each other for the information needed to answer the questions correctly. At the end of a time limit, whoever has the most correct answers wins. Another way would be to have everyone take the test first, and then have each person stand up and give the correct answer as you go down the list of questions. Either way works fine, although the first suggestion is more active and requires more group interaction. A combination of both would be to have everyone take the test first, and then mill around the room asking each person for the correct answers to see if they were right or wrong.

The key is to compose questions that are humorous and interesting and which include "little-known" facts about each person. It's not only fun, but very informative.

Some sample questions:

1. Danny Thompson is saving his money to buy:
   a. A Lear jet
   b. A hair transplant
   c. A moped
   d. A banjo

2. Lisa Burns hates:
   a. sardines
   b. artichokes
   c. cranberries
   d. Danny Thompson

3. Bill Florden's dad once appeared on the Johnny Carson show.
   a. True
   b. False

4. Next Christmas, Paula Lovik's family is going:
   a. to stay home
   b. to Aspen, Colorado
   c. to her grandmother's house in Memphis
   d. crazy

(Contributed by Tom Collins, St. Petersburg, Florida)

MONTEZUMA'S MEMOS

This is a fun (and tasty) crowd breaker that works best with smaller groups. Buy a bag of "Mini-taco" corn chips at the grocery store. They look like Mexican fortune cookies. Then, make up small strips of paper that can be stuffed into the little mini-tacos. On each strip of paper, there is typed a message of some kind. You could put announcements of coming events, crazy stunts that have to be performed on the spot, Bible verses, or whatever. The little strips need to be stuffed into the chips in advance, put in a bowl, and then passed around to the group. Each person takes a turn opening up one of the chips (breaking it), and then reading the message to the group (and doing whatever it says to do, if applicable). Of course, the person may then go ahead and eat the chip.

To add a little excitement to this, you might put a strip of paper in one chip with the words "Montezuma's Revenge" on it. Whoever gets that one gets a penalty of some kind. (Contributed by Don Maddox, Long Beach, California)

Chapter Two

Games

BALANCING BRONCOS

Divide your group into two or more teams. The guys are the horses and the girls are the riders. The object of the game is for a girl to sit cross-legged (Indian-style) on the boy's back. He must go around an obstacle and back without her falling off. If she falls off they must start again at either the beginning or back to the half-way point. The girls can't hang on. They must try to balance. It is easier if they face backwards. If after you divide into teams you have more guys than girls, then the game is over when one team has sent all its guys around the obstacle. (You'll have to use some girls twice.) If the ratio is the other way, then all the girls have to ride. (You'll have to use some boys more than once.) This game moves quickly and is a lot harder than it sounds! (Contributed by Andy Strachan, Keithville, Louisiana)

BANANA WHISTLE

Divide group into three or more teams. Position three people from each team about 20 feet apart as shown in this diagram:

	x			x			x	
		x			x			x
	Team 1			Team 2			Team 3	
	x			x			x	
Starting Line								

A fourth person from each team goes to the starting line and is blindfolded. At a signal, the people positioned on the playing field begin to yell at the blindfolded person trying to get him to come toward them until they can touch him without moving from their positions. This must be done in order (player #1 first, then #2 and #3). At that point the blindfold is removed and the person runs back to the starting line where a fifth person is waiting to feed him a banana. As soon as possible after eating the banana he must whistle an assigned tune as loud as he can for at least 15 seconds. This is good for a lot of laughs and team competition. If there are more people on each team, you can have more than three on the playing field, or they always come in handy for cheering the person on. (Contributed by Brenda Clowers, Bethany, Oklahoma)

BERSERK

Here is a unique game that requires little skill, includes any amount of people and is 100% active. The object is for a group of any size to keep an equal amount of assigned tennis balls moving about a gymnasium floor until six penalties have been indicated.

The vocabulary for this game is unique and essential to the success of the game. It goes like this:

Rabid Nugget: a moving tennis ball
Hectic: a stationary tennis ball
Berserk: a referee's scream, designating a penalty
Frenzy: an elapsed time period measuring six Berserks
Logic: a tennis ball that becomes lodged unintentionally on or behind something
Illogic: a tennis ball that is craftily stuck on or behind something
Paranoia: a player's feeling that the refs are picking on her/him

If thirty players are on the gym floor, thirty *Rabid Nuggets* are thrown, rolled, or bounced simultaneously onto the floor by one of the refs. There are three refs; one at each end of the court and one off to the side at mid-court. It is the duty of the two refs on the floor to try and spot *Hectics* and to generate a hysterical scream (a *Berserk*) so that all will recognize a penalty. The group has five seconds to start a *Hectic* moving again or another full throated *Berserk* is issued. The Berserking ref must point condemningly at the *Hectic* until it is again provided impetus.

Every fifteen seconds after a start the side line ref puts an additional *Rabid Nugget* into play until the final *Berserk* has been recorded.

The team is allowed six *Berserks,* at which juncture the ref on the sidelines, who is responsible for timing this melee, jumps up and down waving his arms yelling STOP—STOP—STOP.

The object is to keep the *Rabid Nuggets* moving as long as possible before six *Berserks* have been recorded. This time span is called a *Frenzy*. After a *Frenzy* ask the group to develop a strategy in order to keep the *Rabid Nuggets* moving for a longer span of time, i.e. increasing the *Frenzy.*

Other Rules:

1. A rabid nugget must be kicked (only kicked) randomly or to another player. It may not be held underfoot and simply moved back and forth.
2. If a rabid nugget becomes a logic or illogic, the ref must get the nugget back into motion. An illogic receives an immediate Berserk.
3. Official tennis balls are not essential to active and satisfying play. You could probably have a heck of a good game if everyone brought their own piece of Silly Putty.
4. There are no official time outs except for double loss of contact lenses or the misfortune of a fractured hang nail.

(Contributed by Karl Rohnke, Ipswich, Massachusetts)

BLACK OUT

Here's a new twist to musical chairs that is a real riot. First arrange the chairs in a circle facing outward. Players form a circle around the outside of the chairs. Explain that players must keep their hands behind their backs. Also explain that the boys must walk around the chairs clock-wise and the girls are to move counter-clock-wise when the music starts or when the whistle blows, etc. When the music stops, participants must sit down on the closest empty chair available. There's one catch, the game is played in the dark. When the music starts have someone turn the lights out. When the music stops the lights go back on. Be prepared for a lot of scrambling, and running for chairs. The person left standing is out. Be sure to take one chair out after each round, and move the remaining chairs closer together as the group gets smaller. Kids have a lot of fun playing this one and usually the girls are more aggressive than the boys. (Contributed by Frank Zolvinski, La Porte, Indiana)

BIBLE FAMILY FEUD

Survey your adult Sunday School class to get their answers to the questions listed below. On the surveys, people are asked to give one answer per question. Then compile your "survey results," rank-ordering all the answers from most to least common, and use these results in a game of "Family Feud" patterned after the popular TV show. It's easiest if you play for games rather than points, like they do on TV. Each team sends a player to the front. The question is

asked of these two players. The player giving the most common response has the option of playing the game or passing it to the player of the other team. The team that plays the game must name all the responses given (or a maximum of the top six responses) without making three mistakes. If they do, they are the winning team. If not, the other team has a chance to "steal" the game if they can name a correct response not named by the other team. The team winning the most games, or best two out of three, etc., is the winner.

Possible Questions:

1. Name a disciple of Jesus.
2. Name one of the Ten Commandments.
3. Name a parable of Jesus.
4. Name a city in Israel.
5. Name a miracle of Jesus.
6. Name one of the fruits of the Spirit.
7. Name one of Paul's letters.
8. Name one of the plaques of Egypt.
9. Name a famous Old Testament character.
10. Name a famous New Testament character.
11. Name one of the spiritual gifts.
12. Name a book of the Old Testament.

(Contributed by Ron Elliott, Bloomington, Minnesota)

BLIND SARDINES

Here's a good game that is not only fun, but encourages community building within the group. There are no "winners" or "losers" in the traditional sense. All you need is a large room and blindfolds for everyone.

One person is appointed (or volunteers) to be the "sardine." The sardine does not wear a blindfold. All the other persons wear blindfolds and their objective is to come into contact with the sardine. When a person wearing a blindfold touches or runs into another person, he asks that person if he is the sardine. The sardine must say yes if touched. Once a person touches the sardine, he must hold onto the sardine for the remainder of the game, so that a chain of people is gradually formed. If a person touches anyone in the chain, it is as if he touched the sardine, and he adds himself to the chain. The sardine must not attempt to avoid being touched by anybody and is free to walk about the room. The game concludes when all are a part of the chain. (Contributed by Thomas M. Church, Bartlesville, Oklahoma)

BOMBS AWAY

For this game, you will need to make a partition out of cardboard or

plywood (or whatever you have handy) that is about five or six feet tall. It should be about the same width, and should have a hole cut in it that is about ten inches in diameter somewhere near the top. The partition can be free-standing, or you can have two people hold it upright on each end while the game is going on.

Next, divide into teams. One person from each team lies down on the floor facing up with his feet toward the partition (under the hole). The rest of the team lines up on the other side of the partition. Each person has a water balloon (or you can use eggs). The object is for players to kneel down on the "tossing line," and to toss the water balloon (or egg) through the hole so that the person lying down on the other side can catch it before it breaks. No warning or signal can be given before tossing the water balloon. The team that has the most unbroken water balloons (or eggs) after every person has tossed (or at the end of a time limit) is the winner. It's a messy game that can be a lot of fun. (Contributed by Brenda Clowers, Bethany, Oklahoma)

CHAIN TAG

Here is a fast-moving game that can be played both indoors or outdoors. It's a game of tag where one person begins as "it," and his job is to catch people (or tag them). When he catches someone then the two of them join hands and continue catching people as a unit. Once there is eight in the group altogether, it breaks apart and becomes two groups of four. This continues with each group of four trying to catch the remaining people. Every time they catch four more, they break off and form a new group of four. The result is several groups of four chasing the free single players who have not been caught yet. The game is played until everyone is caught. Running in groups is a lot of fun and the effect is something like "crack the whip." (Contributed by Joyce Bartlett, Liberty, New Jersey)

CROAK BALL

This is an open field game that is played just like soccer, except that you use an old volleyball and croquet mallets turned sideways. The

kids must *push* the ball with the mallets (no swinging the mallets to hit the ball). Put five to ten kids on each team, mark off goals similar to soccer goals, and make up any other rules that you may find necessary. Each team should have a goalie, but the goalie doesn't have to stay near the goal unless the other team is threatening to score. (Contributed by Dick Moore, Vista, California)

CRUMBLING PYRAMIDS

Divide your teens into groups of six. A team receives points when they are first to complete the instructions given. They must form a complete pyramid and then do the instructions. Following each time they must dismantle and begin when you say "Go!" Scale your points according to the number in the pyramid involved in the action if you make up more instructions.

1. Form a pyramid and say "The Pledge of Allegiance" in unison. (60 points)
2. The "Bottom Person" in the middle must take off his shoes. (20 points)
3. The "two people on the second level" must turn completely around. (40 points)
4. The "person on the top" must comb through both sides of "the person on the bottom left's" hair. (20 points)
5. The "person on the second level on the left" must turn around. (20 points)
6. The "middle person on the bottom" must turn around. (20 points)
7. The whole team turns around in a circle (only the bottom 3 have to move). (60 points)

(Contributed by Andy Strachan, Keithville, Louisiana)

DEAR HUNT

This is a good outdoor game which works best with larger groups at a camp or anywhere there is a lot of room to run around and hide. There are two teams, the boys and the girls. Teams do not have to be even. If the guys outnumber the girls two to one, for example, then you can make the scoring work out so that the girls get more points for each score than the boys do.

The object of the game is to accumulate as many points as possible by "kissing" a member of the opposite team and then having your "kiss" validated at one of the three "Cupid Stations" in your team's territory.

Both teams start off in their own territory (so designated beforehand), which is loosely half the field of play. Once the signal is given to begin, the players begin chasing name members of the opposite team, trying to "kiss" them, which is done by yanking a

name tag (which is a 3x5 card) hanging from their wrist on a piece of string and a rubber band.

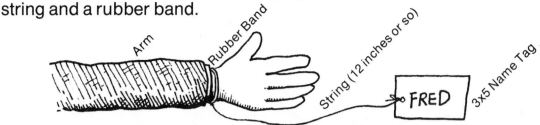

Whoever yanks off the tag first has "kissed" the opposing player and that player must then "faint" (fall down) and cease all activity at that moment. After a few moments, the faint player must rise and go to the "Hospital for the Love Sick" and stay there until he or she is able to gain a "new lease on life." This could be for five minutes or so. A new name tag is made by the resident doctor, and the player is allowed to re-enter the game.

Meanwhile, the player who makes the successful "kiss" continues to "play the field," looking for other prospects and trying to keep from getting kissed by an enemy team member. Once a player has made one or more successful kisses, he or she must get his or her captured tags validated if they are to count toward the team's overall points. This is done by getting to one of three Cupid Stations in their team's area. A Cupid Station is a clearly marked off area where official adult "cupids" wait to validate tags. Once a player is inside a cupid station they are safe from attack—but they can only enter if they have tags that need to be validated. Entering without unvalidated tags causes you to take a "lover's leap" out of the game completely. Tags can only be validated once. Tags are validated by a Cupid signing them on the back and totalling up the combined points and registering these on an official score sheet. If a player fails to make it back to a Cupid Station before getting "kissed," they loose the value of any unvalidated tags they hold.

Certain things are not allowed on the "field of play"—namely holding of any sort, tripping, kicking, or shoving (in general, anything which would not be allowed on a basketball court). Name tags cannot be concealed or held.

There will be adult "chaperones" watching the play. They have automatic authority to call a halt to any illegal activity and to penalize the offending team 50 points for each violation. Failure to heed a warning or prohibition by a chaperone will result in a 300 point penalty and removal from the game of the offending party.

Each validated "Kiss" is worth 20 points. Once the signal is given for the game to end, all persons holding or saving unvalidated tags loose their point value. All Cupids will hand in their score sheets. All Chaperones their penalty cards. From these the total score minus any penalties will be determined. The team with the most points after penalties wins! (Contributed by Phil Kennemer, Elgin, Texas)

FARKLE

The object of this game is to score as much *over* 5000 points as possible by throwing six dice. Points are scored in this manner:

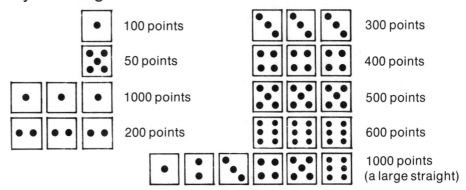

Any three of a kind or large straight must be rolled in one roll, not accumulated in more than one roll. The player starts by rolling all six dice. After rolling, he has the option of ending his turn and adding the score of his dice to his accumulated game score; or putting aside one or more of his dice that score, and rolling the remaining dice. He may continue to do this until he either decides to stop, or scores nothing on the dice he rolls. Any time a player rolls dice and scores nothing on the dice he rolled, he immediately loses his turn and all points accumulated on that turn. This is known as a "Farkle". Whenever he ends up with all six dice scoring points, whether in one turn or in several, he has "turned them over," in which case he may pick all six dice up and roll them again, adding to his accumulated score on that turn, until he chooses to stop or farkles. If he farkles, he loses *all* points accumulated on that turn, including those before he turned them over. Thus, a player's score is not added until he chooses to stop. Once a player sets aside a scoring die or dice, he may not roll them again until he turns over all six dice. A player's *first* score, to get into the game, must be at least 500 on that turn. If he doesn't score 500 points before he farkles, he must try again on his next turn. Play goes around the circle until a player accumulates 5000 or more points. At this point, his game is over, and everyone else has only one more turn—a last chance to pass him. Whoever ends then with the highest score wins.

Farkle is a good party game because any number can play, it's simple, and it promotes conversation. It also tests the balance between a player's greed and good judgment! (Contributed by David Oakes, Albuquerque, New Mexico)

FLIP FLOP HOCKEY

Here's a new way to put a pool table to use if you have one. You only need one billiard ball, and six kids, each armed with one "Flip-Flop" (or "Thong" or "Zorie" or whatever you call those Japanese-style sandals). The heavier Flip-Flops are best. Each player guards one

pocket on the pool table with his Flip-Flop. The game begins when the server serves the ball hitting it with the Flip-Flop. The ball must hit one cushion before any other player touches it. If a player touches it first, the server gets a free shot at that player's pocket. Once the ball is served, any player can hit the ball with his Flip-Flop until it goes into someone's pocket. If you successfully hit the ball into someone else's pocket, you score a point. If someone hits the ball into your own pocket, you lose a point. If there are more than six kids who want to play, have them line up on one end of the table. Then, whenever someone scores a point, rather than the defending player losing a point, he or she is simply knocked out of the game, goes to the end of the line and the next player takes his place.

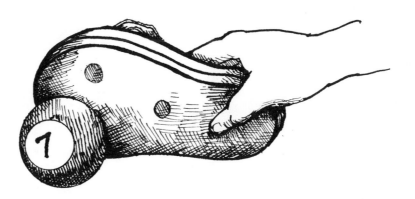

After each point is scored, all players rotate around the table so that everyone has a chance to play all the positions. The game can be played as described above (with each person playing individually), or you can create team competition, with two teams each guarding three pockets. Or you can create a completely new game by changing the rules any way you want. (Contributed by John Davenport, Hemet, California)

GOLFENNIS

This is simply a type of golf game using tennis balls instead of regular golf balls. Provide the kids with plenty of tennis balls, golf clubs (7 irons work best) and an open space (like a golf course, or a football field). You can't play regular golf (tennis balls are too big to go in the little holes, for one thing), but you can play lots of other games this way. For example, you could have a relay race in which teams line up, with half the team on one end of the field, and the other half of the team on the other end of the field, about 100 yards away (see diagram). The first person in line must hit the ball to the first person on the other half of his team as quickly as possible, and then that person returns it back to the original end of the field, and so on until all the players have hit. The first team to complete this task

wins. It's a lot of fun, and when you are in a hurry, a tennis ball hit by a golf club can go anywhere. (Contributed by Doug Larson, Boise, Idaho)

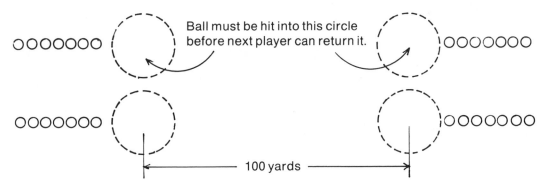

HUMAN FOOTBALL

Here's a wild game that can be played on any rectangular-shaped playing field, outdoors or indoors. A normal football field works fine. There are two teams, the offense and the defense. There can be any number on each team, boys or girls.

When a team is on offense, they begin play at the 20-yard line. They get four downs to move the ball down the field and to score a touchdown. There are no additional first downs. The way yardage is made is for the team on offense to hike the ball to its quarterback, who is then picked up and carried by the rest of the team down the field. The entire team must be joined together, either carrying the quarterback or by holding on to the team members who are carrying the quarterback.

The defensive team begins each play lined up on the goal line which they are defending. As soon as the offensive team hikes the ball, the defensive team locks arms and moves down the field toward the offensive team, now on the move towards them. When the defensive team reaches the offensive team, the two end members of the defense try to dislodge one of the offensive players from the rest of their team. As soon as this is accomplished, the down is over. The ball is then put into play from that point. The defensive team returns to the goal line on each play, and the offensive team repeats the same procedure. If no touchdown is scored in four tries, the defense becomes the offense and gets the ball at the 20 yard line going the other direction. All teams must walk while the ball is in play. If the defense breaks its chain, they must reunite before proceeding down the field. If the offensive chain breaks, the down is automatically over. Score the game any way you wish. (Contributed by Greg Tyree, Yakima, Washington)

KICK THE TIRE

This is simply a game of "kickball," using an old innertube instead of

a rubber ball. Fill the tube quite full, and the pitcher rolls the tube up to home plate, where the kicker gives it a swift kick. It may fly, roll, flop, bounce, no one really knows. The kicker can be put out by a fly that is caught, or if he is hit with the tube enroute to the base. Or you can have force outs, just like regular baseball. Whatever rules you decide to use, this variation of an old game is lots of fun. (Contributed by Glenn Hermann, Richfield, Minnesota)

MARSHMALLOW SURPRISE

At first this game seems mild and old fashioned. You hang a line and on the line you tie marshmallows to strings about 18 inches long. You ask for volunteers to try to eat the marshmallows off the strings without using their hands. When they get up there you ask for volunteers to coach each participant. The coaches must tie blindfolds on each person and back them up about three or four feet from the line. After each person is blindfolded you go over the rules real slow so that another person has enough time to come along with a can of Hershey's chocolate syrup and dip each marshmallow. At a signal the coach verbally directs their person to their marshmallow and tells him or her how close they're getting, etc. The coach must make sure that the participants don't use their hands. Amazingly enough, very few realize that they are making a mess all over their face. The spectators are really getting a good laugh.

Another way to do this is to remove the marshmallows altogether. It's a riot to watch kids hunting with their mouths for something that is not there. Coaches should be clued in. (Contributed by Brenda Clowers, Bethany, Oklahoma)

ODDBALL MIXER

Here's a good mixer or game for almost any size group. Before the game begins, have ten guys and ten girls prepare themselves to fit the descriptions on the lists below. This should be kept somewhat secret until the game begins. Then, give each person a list like those

below. You can use one list for everyone, or you can prepare two separate ones, one for the guys and one for the girls. The idea is simply to try and be the first person to find the people who fit the descriptions and to write in their names. You can make up your own descriptions. The ones given are only suggestions.

For the girls: Find the boy who. . .

1. Has a red comb in his back pocket_____
2. Has a rubber band around his sock_____
3. Has his wrist watch on upside down_____
4. Has his shoes on the wrong feet_____
5. Has a thumb tack in the heel of his right shoe_____
6. Has a bobby pin in his hair_____
7. Has a band-aid on his neck_____
8. Has his shoe laced from the top down_____
9. Has only one sock on_____
10. Has his belt on upside down_____

For the guys: Find the girl who. . .

1. Has one earring on_____
2. Has a rubber band around her wrist_____
3. Has on mis-matched earrings_____
4. Has a penny in her shoe_____
5. Has lipstick on her ear_____
6. Has a paper clip on her collar_____
7. Has nail polish on one fingernail_____
8. Has on one false eyelash_____
9. Is chewing bubble gum_____
10. Has on one nylon stocking_____

(Contributed by Mrs. F. S. Richardett, Howell, New Jersey)

PONY EXPRESS

This is an outdoor game that requires a paved area, bicycles, step-ladders, and the use of water. It's a great game for a warm, sunny day.

Divide into teams of any number, depending on how many bicycles and ladders you have. Form a circular track, with ladders lining the inside of the track (see diagram). Each ladder has a bucket of water on it and a paper cup.

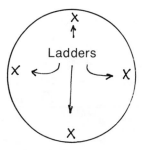

Bike riders are equipped with containers tied to their heads. You can take an old straw hat, turn it upside down and cut slits through it with a scarf through the slits. Tie the scarf under the chin. Line the inside of the hat with plastic and place a plastic bowl in the hat. The straw-hat shaped containers that potted plants come in are perfect. The illustration below might help!

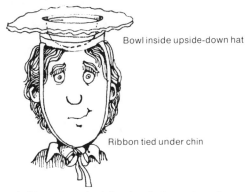

Bowl inside upside-down hat

Ribbon tied under chin

Riders then get on the bicycles (with their hats on) and ride around in the circle as close to the ladders as possible. Teammates are stationed on the ladders, and they try to toss water in the hats of the riders as they ride by. After each lap, the riders dump off their water into a container, and continue until the time limit is up (five minutes is usually sufficient, but it could be longer). Each team goes separately and the team that collects the most water within the time limit is the winner.

If the above procedure seems too complicated, try playing this game with your own set-up. For example, the bike riders could carry water containers on baskets held onto the handlebars, or they could be pulling wagons with buckets in them, or whatever. Use your imagination. You could substitute tricycles for bicycles, or just have the kids run around the circle instead of using bikes. The possibilities are endless. (Contributed by Brenda Clowers, Bethany, Oklahoma)

POT SHOT

Divide the group into two even relay teams. Each team lines up sitting on the floor behind each other with their backs turned toward "the pot" (a toilet seat) at the far end of the two rows. Two "nerf" balls are started at each row. The first person, of each row, takes the ball by clamping the ball between his or her wrists. Still sitting, he turns around to the next person and passes it from his wrists to their wrists, and so on down the line. No hands are used until the ball reaches the last person, then he or she shoots the ball through the pot, with retrievers chasing and throwing back the missed "pot shots." The shooter stays seated and shooting until the shot is made. Then he moves with the ball to the back of the line, the row shifts, and the sequence is repeated until the last person has shot

successfully. Recommended shooting distance is about 5 feet. Players should be spaced about 3 feet apart. (Contributed by Mark Simpson, Everett, Washington)

SEVEN-LEGGED RACE

Divide the kids into two teams. Have everyone pair off with someone of their own team and get into "crab" position. With fabric scraps (they don't hurt) tie a right arm to the left arm of each pair of kids. Have them race relay style to a set place and back again, one pair at a time. The first team to finish wins. (Contributed by Jim Walton, Fitchburg, Massachusetts)

STAR WARS

Here's a game that can generate some excitement simply because of its name. The idea is to cut out dozens (or hundreds) or little cardboard stars about three or four inches wide, and play games with them. One game is to have teams line up behind a foul line and try to toss the stars into a bucket, or onto a chair, or something along those lines. Because of the shape of the stars, they don't always go exactly where they are tossed and it can be a lot of fun. Make up your own rules.

Another game would be to pattern your "Star Wars" game after the game of "Snowfight" (found in an earlier volume of *IDEAS*). Draw a line down the middle of the room, put one team on each side of the line, and give each team an equal number of cardboard stars to begin with. On "go," the object is to throw all your stars onto the opponents "space." At the end of the time limit, the team (or empire) that has the fewest stars on their side of the line is the winner. (Contributed by Jon Hantsbarger, Carthage, Missouri)

SUCK EM UP

Divide the group into three or more teams with equal amounts on each team. Line each team up behind a starting line. Place a paper bucket (like one of those fried chicken buckets or paper paint buckets) about 25-30 feet from the starting line. About two inches from the bottom of the bucket cut a round hole big enough for a ping-pong ball to pass through. Place a ping-pong ball in the

bucket. Position a person at the bucket with a length of plastic plumbing pipe (one inch pipe works best, about 10 inches long).

Back at the starting line place a dish pan full of water in front of each team. Give each team member a straw. At the signal each team member must suck up some water in his straw and hold it in his mouth while he runs to the bucket and puts the water in the bucket. This goes on until the person at the bucket can take the plumbing pipe and blow the ping-pong ball out the hole in the side of the bucket. He then sucks the ball up on the end of the pipe and runs with it to the dish pan at the starting line and drops it in. The first team that gets the ball in their dishpan wins. (Contributed by Brenda Clowers, Bethany, Oklahoma)

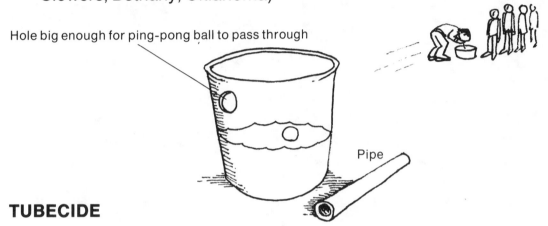

Hole big enough for ping-pong ball to pass through

Pipe

TUBECIDE

This game is most suitably played on a field covered with a glaze of snow. It can, however, be played on any kind of field.

Two equal teams of any size, a field of any size with no boundaries and two large, well-inflated inner tubes are the only requirements for the game. Each team must be given a goal, however. Two markers 15 feet apart will suffice for a goal.

Rules:

1. Two tubes are placed on top of each other in the center of the field. The two teams form a friendly scrum (arms over each other's shoulders in a circle). The entire group yells the word SCRUM three times. On the third SCRUM each team attempts to move their tube towards their goal. Teams are on offense and defense at the same time.
2. When a team gets their tube through their goal, they receive a point. When a goal is scored, play stops for another center SCRUM.
3. The tubes can't be touched with the hands, but it can be forwarded by any other means.
4. Hooking (putting a lag or arm through the tube and holding it) is not allowed.
5. Checking is allowed, but using hands to push or grab is not allowed.

Keep a patch kit and air pump handy. To handicap a group, give them a larger tube. Small tubes are much faster. Feel free to modify the rules as needed to keep the game safe and exciting. (Contributed by Orval Gingerich, Colorado Springs, Colorado)

TURKEY SHOOT

This is a fun little game that you can play next time you take your youth group to an amusement park or to the zoo or to any other place where they divide up into small groups and head out on their own. Give each group about ten "chips" or "tokens" (anything will do) to start with. Then, whenever one group spots another in the park, they yell "Freeze, you Turkey!" at the other group. The spotted group must then surrender one chip to the team that spotted them. At the end of the day, the group that comes back with the most chips wins a prize, or gets the best seats on the bus home, or whatever. It's a lot of fun, and it keeps the kids looking out for each other all day. (Contributed by Rob Moritz, Kansas City, Missouri)

Chapter Three

Creative Communication

ATHEIST ROLE PLAY

This is a simple discussion starter that deals with the question "Does God Really Exist?" Sometimes it's a good idea to force kids to think through their reasons for believing in God (if they say they do) and to strengthen those beliefs. In addition, it is important to take kids a step further and help them to see how their belief (or non-belief) in God makes a difference in the way they live.

Begin with a role play. Have the kids pair off. One person takes the role of an atheist (a person who does not believe in God) and the other is a believer. For about three minutes have the kids assume these roles and try to convince the other person that their view is the correct one. After they have done this, have another person (like one of the youth sponsors) come before the entire group and take the position of an atheist. The group must try to convince him that he is wrong. Since the kids have had some practice in their individual role plays, they should be well equipped to do so.

The next step is to give the kids pencil and paper, and to ask them to write down five things that would change in their lives if they knew for certain that there was no God. What difference would it make in the way they lived? Next, have them write down five things that would probably change in their lives if they knew for a fact that there really was a God. In other words, how would their lives be different from the way they are now if God somehow made himself known (by appearing in the sky, or something like that) so that there was absolutely no doubt whatsoever that He existed. How would they behave differently?

Now have the kids compare their lists and discuss the differences between both lists and the way they live right now.

Follow this up with a discussion. Some possible questions:

1. On the basis of arguments presented, etc., do you believe in God or not? (You might have a vote, secret ballot if you want.)
2. Is it possible to "abstain" in a vote for or against the existence of God? In other words, can a person just not have an opinion? What are the consequences of such a position?
3. How does how you believe affect the way you live right now?

(Contributed by Ken Potts, La Grange, Illinois)

BIGGER AND BETTER TALENT HUNT

This is a game that can lead into a learning experience based on the Parable of the Talents (Matthew 25:14-30). The game is the "Bigger and Better Hunt" (previously described in *IDEAS Number Four*).

Begin by dividing into groups of three or four per group. Then give each group a certain amount of money. It could be a penny, or it could be a dollar. The amount doesn't matter too much. The task of each group is to go into the neighborhood and try to trade the money for something of value, and then to continue trading with the purpose of increasing the value each time. In other words, they might begin by going to someone's house and asking them if they had anything that they would be willing to sell (or trade) for the penny (or whatever amount they were starting with). After making the deal, they then go to another house and try to sell that item for more money, or trade it up for something else. The group should have thirty minutes to an hour to work with, and the group that comes back at the end of the time with the most value (either in money or merchandise) is the winner. Kids may not add any of their own money to the total, nor may they solicit donations. The only acceptable method of acquiring more value is through trading.

After the game, follow up with a discussion of what happened. Was it hard to do? How did you approach it? Did some methods work better than others? Did you ever want to just stop at one point and not go any further? Move into a study of the Parable of the Talents and see if the kids are able to understand it better after having played the game. Wrap up with a few thoughts on the importance of taking what God has given to us and putting forth every effort to invest those gifts into meaningful service as opposed to "hiding them under a bushel." Point out that the parable takes the emphasis off of "how many" talents were given and places the emphasis on the amount of effort each person puts into multiplying those talents. (Contributed by Ruth Staal, Grand Rapids, Michigan)

COLORADO OR NEW YORK?

This is an exercise that is fun to do and gets people to think about who they are and what they value. It is also a good community-builder as it helps to open a group up to each other in a non-threatening way.

Print up and pass out the "I AM MORE LIKE. . ." list (below) to each person asking them to circle one word after each number that they feel they are most like (not that they would rather be). Tell them to circle the one they would most often feel like or choose. Ask them to think of the analogy between each of the two items, or of what connotations it would bring to their minds as they try to decide

between the two. Explain that one item is not necessarily better than the other, only different.

For example, on item #1, the choice is between Colorado and New York. These two places bring to mind two distinctive environments or personalities. The idea on this one is not necessarily to choose your favorite place, or which one you would rather visit, but which one you are most like. Maybe you are "most like" New York because you have a lot of things going on in your life, or because you are loud and boisterous, or because you are an exciting person. Or you may be more like Colorado, because you see yourself as quiet and alone, or majestic and solid (like the Rocky Mountains), or as clean, uncluttered, or refreshing. Got the idea?

Here is the list to be distributed to the group:

I AM MORE LIKE. . .

1. Colorado. . .New York
2. Volkswagen. . .Mercedes Benz
3. A leaky faucet. . .an overflowing dam
4. Moonlight. . .Firelight
5. Led Zepplin. . .Kenny Rogers
6. The Mountains. . .The Desert
7. Marathon runner. . .Sprinter
8. Silk. . .Flannel
9. Dove. . .Eagle
10. Tug boat. . .Sailboat
11. Easy chair. . .Wood bench
12. Oil Painting. . .Snapshot
13. River. . .Lake
14. Paved highway. . .Rocky road
15. Hand. . .Eye
16. Lock. . .Key
17. Filing cabinet. . .Bulletin board
18. Tire. . .Steering Wheel
19. Arrow. . .The Bow
20. Music. . .The Dancer
21. Collector. . .Dispensor
22. Golfer. . .Sky Diver
23. Checkbook. . .Treasure Chest
24. Social worker. . .Business executive
25. House. . .Tent
26. Fall. . .Spring
27. Jaguar. . .Snail
28. Violin. . .Trumpet
29. Morning. . .Evening
30. Wax. . .Rock
31. Cream Cheese. . .Hot Sauce
32. Comedian. . .Lawyer
33. Coal. . .Diamond
34. Lamb. . .Fox
35. News Report. . .Soap Opera
36. Politician. . .Philosopher

After everyone has completed the exercise, go over each number and have the kids raise their hands if they feel they are more like the first item than the second. Then have those who feel they are more like the second item also raise their hands. Have them discuss the analogies they saw between the two items, and give them the opportunity to share why they picked the item they did.

Some questions for further discussion:

1. Do you ever feel threatened when you discover that your values are different from someone elses? Why? Do you think that God wants us to all have the same values, tastes, personalities, and so forth?
2. Do you think that some of the choices on the list have a "more Christian" response than others?
3. How did your interpretation of the items on the list make a difference in which one you chose? What does this say to us about the value of communication, and trying to understand each other better? Can another person's interpretation be just as right as your own? What does interpretation and first impressions have to do with the way we accept and relate to others?
4. After this exercise, are there certain items that you would like to change? Are you unsatisfied with how you see yourself right now? What can a person do to change?
5. How does our own self-awareness (how we see ourselves) affect the way we relate to others? How we relate to God?

(Contributed by Anna Hobbs, Santee, California)

CREATION, GOD, AND YOU

This exercise and discussion is great for camps and retreats, but it can be used almost anywhere. Begin by giving each person a piece of paper and pencil. Take them outside and have them list all the things they notice about nature—the things it does or is like. (For example, the great variety of colors, the intricacy of plant structure, the sun that heats the earth, enabling life to exist, and so on.)

When the time is up, have the group return and share their results with the rest of the group. After this, ask them to describe the most scenic spot they have ever visited or where they think the most beautiful place in the world is, or what it is about creation that amazes them the most. Use this as a take-off to find out what Scripture has to say about God who created it all.

Have different people read the following passages:

Genesis 1:4, 1:26, 2:7   Hebrews 11:3
Romans 1:19-20, 8:21-23   Revelation 4:1

After each passage, have someone briefly state in their own words, what the basic idea of the passage was.

Lead the group in discussion, using the following questions as a way of getting at God's character expressed through His creation. Tell the group to use the Scripture just read and other Scripture as a basis from which to think about and answer the questions.

1. What are some things we know about God upon observing His creation? Can you list some of His attributes?
2. Is creation an extension of God or is creation something separate from God?
3. In the beginning God looked at creation and said it was good Is it still good? Did the "Fall" make it bad?
4. What is the purpose of creation?
5. Is creation still going on? Is God still involved in His creation? Explain.
6. How does creation speak to us in a personal way? Can you name some things that would be relevant to your own personal situation? How does our knowledge of God through creation help us to trust Him?

(Contributed by Anna Hobbs, Santee, California)

THE CRUTCH WALKERS

The following parable is based on the idea that to some people Christianity is only a "crutch." Read it to the group and then discuss the questions that follow.

There existed a planet on which all the inhabitants were unable to walk. They crawled through life not knowing the pleasure of viewing life upright with the easy mobility of walking. History said that many years before the descendants had been able to use their legs effectively and walk upright without crawling or pulling their bodies with their hands as they did now.

One day a person came among them who showed great love and compassion toward them. He told them that not only had their descendants walked on their legs, but that this was possible for them too. He offered crutches for those who believed him, with the promise that someday, if they trusted him, by using their crutches they would be able to walk upright even without them.

Some of the people decided to try the crutches. Once they were upright they found how much larger their world became because of this new ease in mobility. They encouraged everyone to join them in this new found freedom.

Others doubted the crutch walkers would ever be free of their crutches and be able to walk alone. They scoffed at them and said, "We are satisfied with life as we live it. We don't need the assistance of a crutch to experience life. Only the weak need the aide of crutches to get around!"

Questions for discussion:

1. If you were one of the people in the story, would you have tried

the crutches? Why or why not?

2. Why do you think some people did not want to try the crutches, and put other people down who did?
3. Do you feel that Christianity is only a "crutch?" If so, in what way? Is this good or bad?
4. How would you respond to a person who rejected Christianity because they thought that it was "only a crutch?"

You might wrap up with some thoughts on the importance of realizing that we are in fact handicapped without Christ, and that it is only when we admit that we are crippled that we are able to walk. Some applicable Scripture might include II Corinthians 12:10, Numbers 21:4-9, John 3:14-16, and John 1:9-12. (Contributed by Bill and Sheila Goodwin, Kalamazoo, Michigan)

DATING QUIZ

Here's a good quiz that can generate a lot of discussion on the subject of dating. After the group has a chance to finish it, go over each question and compare answers.

Circle the best answer:

As a Christian, I may date. . .
   a. non-Christians
   b. non-Christians, but only casually
   c. non-Christians only if they are unusually attractive
   d. any Christian
   e. only "strong" Christians
   f. "Weak" Christians as a ministry
   g. only unusually attractive Christians

It is "more Christian" to...
   a. play the field
   b. only date one person at a time

It is "more Christian" to. . .
   a. wait for a mate until God brings one into your life
   b. go out "hunting" for one if one does not appear (even attending a school where prospects look good)

It is "more Christian"...
   a. for one's parents to pick his or her mate
   b. for me to pick my own mate
   c. to marry a "computer date"
   d. to marry someone you meet at a church conference

It is "more Christian" to. . .
   a. date for companionship
   b. only date someone you might be "serious" about

Finish the sentence:

When you realize that someone you are dating cares much more for you than you do for them, you should. . .

If, as a Christian, you never have any dates and would like some, you should. . .

My pet peave about dating is. . .

Biblical principles I think apply to dating are. . .

Some lessons I've learned about dating are. . .

Prevalent dating practices which I feel are basically non-Christian are. . .

(Contributed by Dan Mutschler, Chicago, Illinois)

DATING QUIZ II

Here are some more good questions on the subject of dating which could be added to or substituted for the questions in the preceding quiz. Again, the idea is not to get the "correct" answer (note that there is no answer key), but simply to generate discussion.

1. I go on a date because. . .
   a. I like to see the latest movies
   b. I enjoy spending my parents' money
   c. I like being broke Sunday through Friday
   d. It gives me something else to do besides homework

2. I select a date by. . .
   a. seeing if he/she is well dressed
   b. hearing whether he/she is a "fun date"
   c. I want to become romantically involved with he/she
   d. all the above

3. Where I go on a date is determined by. . .
   a. the amount of money I have, or the amount that I want to spend
   b. how far my date will let me
   c. where my parents will let me
   d. where my friends are

4. I do not like to double date because...
   a. I do not like to hear unintelligible noises coming from the back seat
   b. we can never all agree where to go, so we drive around a lot
   c. the "other couple" always has bad breath
   d. one of us has to ride with the other two after one of the dates is dropped off

5. I do not date people my own age because. . .
    a. we have nothing in common
    b. he/she still sucks their thumb
    c. they are "all taken"
    d. it's hard to talk with a gorilla

6. I only date "Christian" people because. . .
    a. we both can say God without becoming embarrassed
    b. he/she may keep their hands off me longer
    c. my parents approve
    d. we can pray on our date

7. I never date the same person twice because. . .
    a. he always goes to the same place
    b. I told him that I don't kiss on the first date
    c. the weather forecast is the same for this weekend
    d. I'm afraid we might get involved

8. I never spend much money on a date because. . .
    a. I am saving it for college
    b. she's not worth it
    c. I spent it all on Wednesday night with the "boys"
    d. it has to last me the rest of the month

9. I do not date because. . .
    a. I have no money
    b. nobody has called
    c. she might say no if I ask
    d. I have a case of terminal zits and donkey breath

10. Dating is fun because. . .
    a. I like to dance
    b. I like to get stepped on
    c. I get to mess around
    d. I get out of the house

TRUE/FALSE

1. You should never hold hands on a date, it may lead to more dangerous things.
2. The boy should ask the parents (preferably the father) for permission to date their daughter.
3. To date someone is to look for a potential marriage partner.
4. You should only date Christian people.
5. I like to date someone because they have a pleasant personality.
6. It does not matter how much money was spent on the date so long as we had a good time.
7. I could feel closer to her if she did not bring her pet doberman with her on our date.

8. I like seeing explicit sexual scenes, both at the movies and in the other cars around us.
9. You should always pray (not prey) on a date.
10. I like having my parents drive us on our date.

(Contributed by Joe Dorociak, Memphis, Tennessee)

EASTER CROSSWORD

Here is a crossword puzzle that tests a group's knowledge of the events leading up to Easter. It can be printed up and done individually, or it can be done as a group game.

Instructions (When done as a group game):

Divide the group into two teams. Teams may elect (or be assigned) to go either "across" or "down." There are an equal number of clues, and it is doubtful that there would be any advantage to being either "across" or "down." There are two (possibly three) rounds in the game. During round one, each team gets a clue (in order) to a word in their section of the puzzle and will get 100 points for each correct answer. The questions (clues) can be given to individuals on the teams, or to the entire team, whichever you decide. Once the answer is given, it cannot be changed, but wrong answers are not written in the puzzle. Alternate questions between the "across" and "down" teams until you have gone through the entire puzzle one time.

During round two, the missed clues are given again in the same fashion, only this time correct answers are worth 50 points. If there are still empty spaces on the puzzle, then go ahead with round three, awarding 25 points for correct answers this time. Also, Scripture references and Bibles may be provided during this round.

A good way to conduct the game would be to make a large poster of the puzzle that could be seen by everyone, or make an overhead transparency of it. Do not give the teams the list of clues in advance.

Clues:

ACROSS

6. Luke's gospel emphasizes Jesus' humanity by calling Him the "_____ of man."
9. This Jewish leader helped prepare Jesus' body for burial (John 19:39).
11. High Jewish priest at the time of the crucifixion (Matthew 26:3).
12. The Jews also wanted to kill this man because he'd been risen from the dead (John 12:10).
13. The man who carried Christ's cross (Luke 23:26).
14. This ripped from top to bottom upon Jesus' death (Matthew 27:51).
18. High council of Jewish leaders (Mark 15:1, NASV, cross-reference).
19. Natural disaster which occurred when Jesus died (Matthew 27:54).
22. Jesus was His only begotten Son (John 3:16).
23. Wealthy Jewish leader who gave His own tomb to Jesus (Matthew 27:59, 60).

26. The "blood money" paid to Judas was eventually used to purchase this burial place for strangers (Matthew 27:6-10).
27. Woman who annointed Jesus with expensive perfume (John 12:3).
28. He caused Judas to betray Christ (Luke 22:3).
29. The disciple who doubted Christ's resurrection (John 20:24, 25).
31. Jesus said He would rebuild this in three days (Mark 14:58).
35. This Old Testament prophet foretold the sufferings of Christ (Isaiah 53).
37. These were fashioned into a crown for Jesus to wear by Roman soldiers (John 19:5).
38. Roman governor who passed the death sentence on Christ (Mark 15:15).
40. The day of Jesus resurrection.
42. Jesus died for _____.
45. Peter was observed in this location when Jesus was taken by the mob (John 18:26).
46. Notorious prisoner released to Jews by Pilate (Mark 15:7-11).
49. Animal which signaled Peter's denial of Jesus (John 18:27).
50. Jesus performed this service for the disciples in the Upper Room (John 13).
51. Gospel writer who devotes the greatest number of chapters to Jesus' last days (John 12-21).
52. Jesus compared His three days in the tomb to the plight of this Old Testament character (Matthew 12:40).
53. He was chosen by lot to replace Judas among the twelve (Acts 1:26).
54. This is a symbol of Christ's body, broken for us (I Corinthians 11:24).
55. The crime which Jesus was accused by the Jews (Matthew 26:65).

DOWN

1. The cry of the multitudes during Jesus' triumphal entry to Jerusalem (Matthew (21:9).
2. Jesus' purpose in going to the Mount of Olives after the Last Supper, to _____ (Luke 22:40, 41).
3. "This is My _____ which is given for you; this do in remembrance of Me." (Luke 22:19).
4. Roman soldier at the crucifixion who became convicted of Christ's deity (Mark 15:39).
5. In Gethsemane, Jesus prayed to have this taken from Him (Mark 14:36).
7. Signal used by Judas to betray Christ (Matthew 26:49).

8. Occupation of the two men hung with Jesus (Matthew 27:38).
10. Type of branches cast before Jesus as He entered Jerusalem (John 12:13).
11. Christian sacrament which began with the Last Supper.
15. These were cast by soldiers to divide Christ's clothes (Mark 15:24).
16. First person to see the resurrected Christ (Mark 16:9, John 20:11-18).
17. _____ pieces of silver, the price paid to Judas (Matthew 26:15).
20. "The place of a skull" (where Jesus was crucified) (Mark 15:22).
21. Peter cut an ear off this slave of the high priest (John 18:10).
24. Disciple who denied Christ three times (Luke 21:61).
25. Book of Bible which records Jesus' ascension to heaven (Acts 1:9).
26. The "Feast of Unleavened Bread" (Mark 14:1).
30. Jesus was made to be this for us, that we might become righteous (II Corinthians 5:21).
32. Jesus' crucifixion was part of God's _____ of salvation.
33. The resurrected Jesus appeared to two men on the way to this village (Luke 24:13-15).
34. Christ did this for the bread and wine (Luke 22:17, 19).
36. Setting of the Last Supper (Luke 22:12).
39. Animal which was sacrificed at the Feast of Unleavened Bread (Mark 14:12).
41. Roman soldiers dressed Jesus in this garment of scarlet and mocked Him (Matthew 27:28).
42. Young follower of Jesus (later a gospel writer) who ran away without his clothes when he was seized by the mob in the garden (Mark 14:51, 52).
43. The king of Judea who was in Jerusalem at the time of the crucifixion (Luke 23:8-12).
44. Jesus entrusted the care of His mother to this man (John 19:26, 27).
47. Animal which carried Jesus on His entry to Jerusalem (John 12:15).
48. Name for Jesus which means "teacher" or "master" (Mark 14:45).

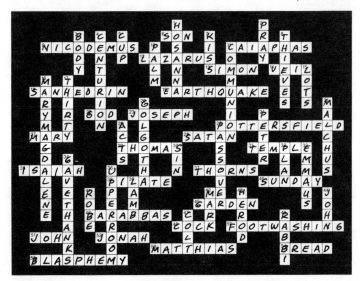

(Contributed by Barbara Martin, Delta, Ohio)

EASTER I.Q. TEST

Here is a great little quiz that can be used in conjunction with a Bible study on Easter, or simply to test a group's knowledge of the Easter story as it is presented in Scripture.

Instructions: Place an "x" on the line if you think the answer is Biblically correct:

1. The woman (or women) who went to the tomb was (or were):
_____*a. Mary Magdalene and the other Mary*
_____*b. Mary Magdalene, Mary the mother of James, & Salome*
_____*c. Mary Magdalene, Mary the mother of James, Joanna & others*
_____*d. Mary Magdalene*

2. The time of early morning was:
_____a. when the sun had risen
_____b. while it was still dark

3. At the tomb was (or were):
_____a. an angel
_____b. a young man
_____c. two men
_____d. two angels

4. The reaction of the woman (or women) was one of:
_____a. amazement, astonishment
_____b. fear and trembling
_____c. great joy

5. After leaving the tomb, the woman (or women):
_____a. told the disciples
_____b. said nothing to anyone

6. The reaction of the disciples at first was that:
_____a. they did not believe the women; it seemed an idle tale
_____b. Peter & John went immediately & quickly to the tomb

7. Jesus first appeared to the disciples:
_____a. in Galilee, on a mountain
_____b. in an upper room in Jerusalem

8. Jesus seemingly last appeared to the disciples:
_____a. on a mountain in Galilee
_____b. on a mountain in Bethany (or just outside Bethany)
_____c. by the Sea of Tiberias

9. The gift of the Holy Spirit was given to the disciples:
_____a. before Jesus ascended; in the upper room he breathed on them
_____b. after Jesus ascended, on the Day of Pentecost

10. We have many details about the crucifixion and death of Jesus. Which Gospel writer gives the most details about the actual Resurrection of Jesus from the grave? Which one best describes what happened when Jesus rose from the dead?
_____a. Matthew
_____b. Mark
_____c. Luke
_____d. John

The answers are found in Matthew 28, Mark 16, Luke 24, John 20-21, and Acts 1. In questions 1 through 9, all of the choices are correct, and in question 10, none are correct, since none of the Gospels describe the actual Resurrection of Christ; only what happened afterward. Obviously this quiz can open up some good discussion on the differences between the four Gospel accounts and how they can be reconciled to each other. (Contributed by Tim Spilker, Lakeside, California)

HOW MANY F'S?

Here is a fun little experiment that can be tied in quite nicely with a lesson on awareness. Print up some sheets like the one below and give one to each person in the group face down. Everyone turns the page over and begins at the same time. Each person should work alone.

Read the following sentence in the enclosed block. After reading the sentence, go back and count the F's. You have <u>one</u> minute.

```
FINISHED FILES ARE THE RE-
SULT OF YEARS OF SCIENTIF-
IC STUDY COMBINED WITH
THE EXPERIENCE OF YEARS.
```

Number of F's in the block _____

Try it yourself before you read the answer below.

Most people will count three. Others will see four or five. Only a few will count all six F's that are in the box. After the 30 seconds are up, ask the group how many F's they counted, and you will get a variety of answers. Those who counted only three, four, or five will be quite surprised when you tell them the answer. But after they find all six F's, they will feel rather silly that they didn't see them in the first place. Most people tend to overlook the word "OF" when they are counting. This is because they are looking only at the bigger words.

This test is often given to people in driving classes to demonstrate how we often fail to see motorcycles on the road because they are so small, and because we aren't looking for them. After they are pointed out, they become obvious. This lesson can also be applied to people. We often miss the good qualities in other people because we aren't looking for them. We tend to look instead for the things that we want to see—the bad things. This is to make ourselves look good by comparison.

Follow up on this idea with an exercise like "What Others Think Of Me" (in *IDEAS Number Eleven*) in which kids look for the good in each other, and affirm each other's gifts and abilities. It's amazing how when these things are pointed out, they then become more obvious. It also does a lot for everyone's self-esteem.

IDENTITY MASKS

Get some large grocery sacks. Cut out a slot in each sack for the eyes so that it might be used as a mask over the head. On the sacks, write (in red) different identities adolescents get in high school. Under these names, write down (in black) how they are to be treated.

Give each person one of these masks, face down so that they don't know what is on it. Have the kids shut their eyes and put the masks on for them so they cannot see who they are. Tell them to mill around the room and interact with each other. They have two tasks: to treat each person according to the directions on the masks, and to guess who they are from the interaction of others with them. Tell them to keep in touch with their feelings, especially their feelings about themselves. (For best results: give the negative labels to the most outgoing, accepted kids in the group and the positive labels to the quieter, less noticed ones.)

Here are some ideas for masks (be creative with others):

Joe Cool   -ask me to parties
           -accept me
           -laugh at all I say
           -tell me how cool I am

Patty Party   -invite me to any social gathering
              -accept me
              -act wild and uninhibited around me

Betty Bod   -ask me out
            -accept me
            -flirt with me
            -tell me how good looking I am

Jerry Jock   -tell me how strong I am
             -talk about sports around me
             -flirt with me
             -ask me to be on your sports team

Ivan Intellect   -respect me for my "smarts"
                 -ask me to sit by you in class
                 -tell me how intelligent I am

Steven Stud   -ask me out
              -tell me how good looking I am
              -flirt with me
              -accept me—get in good with me

Bryan Bookworm   -reject me
                 -tell me I'm boring
                 -poke fun at me

Ralph Runt   -kid me about being small
             -reject me subtly
             -act big around me

Andy Clutz   -reject me
             -tell about the dumb things I do
             -tell a joke about me

Paul Problem   *-feel sorry for me*
                -tell me how you understand
                -ask me if it's going better today
                -don't respect me

Susie "Dumb" Blonde   *-treat me as spacy*
                       -but flirt with me

Nelson Nerd   *-reject me*
               -make nasty remarks to me
               -make fun of me

Wanda Wallflower   *-reject me—don't acknowledge me*
                    -don't speak to me even if I talk

Ms. Liberation   *-accept me*
                  -tell me how good I am in sports
                  -act free around me
                  -but don't ask me out or tell me I'm pretty

Ted Tough Guy   *-act afraid of me*
                 -ask me if I've heard any off-color jokes lately
                 -try to get on my good side
                 -ask me to help you "get even" with somebody

After the kids have had a chance to mingle long enough for their new personalities to form, discuss how who we are comes from others' opinions of us. Discuss also how labels are not our real selves—people try to hang their trips on us. Then show God's view of us and how His opinion of us is the one which should shape our lives. (Contributed by Gary Salyer, Anderson, Indiana)

LEGALISM STROLL

This is a good exercise that helps young people to understand that a legalist approach to the Christian life is not feasible. It can be used to compare and contrast righteousness under the law and righteousness under grace.

The basic idea is for kids to follow a strip of tape through the church (or whatever area you have available), walking on the tape with both feet, being careful not to leave the "straight and narrow" path. Stationed along the line at various points are numerous "temptations" (set up by the youth sponsors) that are designed to get the kids to leave the line. Some of these can be pleasurable things designed to lure them away, and other things can incorporate the use of scare tactics. Kids are told at the outset that their task is to stay on the tape, and if they do (without ever stepping off of it), there will be a reward for them at the end of the tape.

Temptations along the way can include the following:

1. Someone shooting at them with a squirt gun at a certain point, making them mad or uncomfortable.
2. The youth director can sit in a chair about twelve feet away from the line, and there can be a pile of water balloons just out of arms' reach of the kids. The youth director dares anyone to try and hit him with a water balloon. (But they have to leave the line in order to do it.)
3. At one point, you can try to persuade kids that you need their help to lure someone else off the line.
4. Someone dressed as a monster can jump out and scare them off the line.
5. Place cookies, punch, candy, etc. on the table just out of reach of the line. Leave the table unattended, but have someone watching from a hidden position.
6. At one point, kids can be told by a youth sponsor that the game has been terminated, that they don't need to follow the line anymore. The whole thing was just a joke and there isn't really a reward for them.

You can think of other ideas for temptations or tactics designed to get them to stray from the straight and narrow. Some of them will work, and some of them won't. There will undoubtedly be some kids who proceed right along the line without leaving it, but many will succumb to temptation somewhere along the way. This will lead into an excellent discussion on the topics previously described. Try to relate the various temptations to actual or real temptations that we face all the time. For example, when they are told that the game is over (when it wasn't), they will cry foul because they were lied to, but this can be tied in with the idea that Satan is a liar. Wrap up with a discussion on the impossibility of living a perfect life (or staying on the line forever), and how Christ has provided us with another, better way. (Contributed by Les Palich, Manhattan, Kansas)

LET THERE BE LIGHT

This is a good discussion experience that is also effective for a

worship time together. It should be done at night (or in a room that can be darkened), and it is best with smaller groups. You will need candies and Bibles.

The group sits on the floor in a circle. Explain at the beginning that they will be doing the teaching themselves. The subject is "light". Ask them to spend a few minutes looking up passages in Scripture that deal with light. They may help each other, or they can use Bible concordances, etc. to help them find Scripture that talks about light in some way. (Take as long as you need for this.) Tell the group that they will need to memorize the passage, or at least the thought, as they may not have enough light to read.

Now turn out the light, making it as dark as possible. Give each person an un-lit candle. Have each person go around the circle and say something about darkness. This can be a definition of darkness or just a statement about what darkness reminds them about.

Next, light one candle, telling the group that they will pass the flame around the circle from candle to candle. As the flame is passed around, each person is to share what they have discovered in their research that the Bible says about light. They can quote their passage or comment on the meaning of the passage. They then light the candle of the next person, who also shares. Do this until everyone's candle is lit. You as the leader can then wrap-up any way you want. The result is usually very meaningful. (Contributed by Jerry Martin, Costa Mesa, California)

LETTERS TO JESUS

Many young people feel inadequate or awkward when praying out loud in front of a group. They don't do it very often, so they really feel intimidated when they are asked to pray, even though they may want to. This exercise is designed to help overcome some of those fears. Have the group imagine that they are writing a letter to Jesus. Give them pencils, paper, and some idea of what the letter should include.

For example, the letter should begin with greetings and perhaps some thank yous. Thank Him for something personal. Thank Him for someone or something and tell why. Share with Him some experiences you've had lately, when you felt happy, and when you felt lousy. Share with Him some of your concerns and worries. If you have any requests, mention those somewhere in your letter, as well.

After the kids have had time to write their letters, explain that these letters are just like prayers, and that God actually does get them. You might want to go around the groupand share the letters with each other. Of course, kids should be allowed to pass if they want to. You might suggest that reading them out loud (either in the group, or

at home privately) is the same as "mailing" the letters. (Contributed by Billy King, Weatherford, Oklahoma)

LOVE MESSAGE TO A LOST WORLD

Here's an idea that would be especially appropriate around Valentine's Day. Tell the kids you want them to create a love message that will give hope to a lost world; (or tell them that you want them to create a message to someone they've been wanting to tell about Jesus Christ) and do it in the form of a card (like a Valentine's card) or on a poster. Give them the option of working in pairs or alone.

Make available lots of construction paper in various colors (especially red and white), poster board, ribbon, scissors, markers, crayons, paste, aluminum foil, craft sticks, poster paint, brushes, colored chalk, etc. Also, provide Bibles and perhaps song books to help stimulate thinking.

After everyone is finished give them time to share what they have done. Then put them up in a prominent place to be shared with the church family. (As with any creative activity, only display them if the kids give their permission.)

If they feel good about the cards, suggest they make them and give them to someone they know who is not a Christian. (Contributed by L. Dean Jones, Indianapolis, Indiana)

NOAH AND THE ARK I.Q. TEST

Here's a fun little quiz that works great as a way to generate new interest in the old familiar story of Noah and the Ark. Most people assume that they know most everything about the facts of the story, but this test may prove otherwise.

1. Why did God decide to destroy all living things with the flood?
   a. Because Israel was disobedient.
   b. Because the Romans were corrupt and needed to be punished.
   c. Because everyone was wicked and evil.
   d. Because He knew it was the only way to get rid of disco-dancing and junk food.

2. Why did God pick Noah to survive the Flood?
   a. Noah was the only guy around who knew how to build an ark.
   b. Noah was the only guy around who loved God and would obey Him.
   c. Noah won the trip in a sweepstakes.
   d. Noah begged God to save himself and his family.

3. What was Noah's profession?
   a. Animal expert
   b. Boat builder
   c. Farmer
   d. Temple priest

4. How did Noah find out about the coming flood?
   a. He read about it in the Bible.
   b. He had a dream about it.
   c. He was notified by a prophet.
   d. God told him.

5. How long did Noah have to build the ark and get ready for the flood after he found out about it?
   a. 40 days
   b. One year
   c. Three years
   d. 120 years

6. What were the names of Noah's three sons?
   a. Ham, Shem, and Japheth
   b. Ham, Sam, and Jeff
   c. Ham, Turkey, on Rye
   d. Huey, Dewey, and Louie

7. How old was Noah when his three sons were born?
   a. In his twenties
   b. In his thirties
   c. About 60 years old
   d. About 500 years old

8. How big was the ark?
   a. 50 cubits high, 30 cubits wide, and 300 cubits long
   b. 300 cubits long, 30 cubits high, and 50 cubits wide
   c. 300 cubits wide, 50 cubits long, and 30 cubits high
   d. About the size of the Queen Mary

9. How long is a cubit?
   a. About the same as three schmuckos
   b. About 2.5 meters
   c. About the length of one's forearm
   d. About a yard (three feet)

10. How many doors did the ark have?
    a. One
    b. Two (One on the side, and one on top)
    c. Just the one on the captain's quarters
    d. Who knows?

11. How many floors did the ark have?
    a. One
    b. Three
    c. It was a ranch-style, split-level ark
    d. Who knows?

12. How many people did Noah take on the ark with him?
    a. Three
    b. Seven
    c. Eleven
    d. Thirteen

13. True or False: Noah took only two of each species with him on the ark?
    a. True
    b. False

14. How old was Noah when the flood came?
    a. 35
    b. 50
    c. 120
    d. 600

15. Where did the flood waters come from?
    a. A broken pipe
    b. From the sky
    c. From inside the earth
    d. Both b and c

16. How long did the flood last?
    a. A little over a year
    b. 40 days and 40 nights
    c. About three months
    d. Who knows?

17. What bird did Noah send out first to see if there was dry land?
    a. A pigeon
    b. A raven
    c. A chicken
    d. A sparrow
    e. None of the above

18. What did the dove return with the first time Noah sent it out?
    a. A pepperoni pizza
    b. Nothing
    c. An olive leaf
    d. An olive branch
    e. An olive pit

19. What did the dove return with the last time Noah sent it out?
    a. Olive Oyl
    b. A message of peace
    c. Nothing
    d. It did not return

20. Where is the story of Noah in the Bible?
    a. The book of Genesis
    b. The book of Exodus
    c. The book of Noah
    d. The book of Moses

21. After the flood was over, what did Noah do?
    a. He continued his righteous life, never sinning again.
    b. He planted a vineyard.
    c. He got drunk.
    d. He opened a boat store.
    e. Both b and c.

22. God sent a rainbow as a way of saying to Noah:
    a. "There's a pot of gold at the end of every rainbow."
    b. "Somewhere over the rainbow."
    c. "Every cloud has a silver lining."
    d. "You don't have to worry about floods anymore, Noah."
    e. "Don't forget what happened Noah. Next time it will be worse!"

23. True or False: Recent scientific expeditions have found remains of the ark on Mt. Sinai.
    a. True
    b. False
    c. Maybe

Answers:

 1. c (Gen. 6:11-13)
 2. b (Gen. 6:9, 7:1)
 3. c (Gen. 9:20)
 4. d (Gen. 6:17)
 5. d (Gen. 6:3, 7:6)
 6. a (Gen. 6:10)
 7. d (Gen. 5:32)
 8. b (Gen. 6:15)
 9. c
10. a (Gen. 6:16)
11. b (Gen. 6:16)
12. b (Gen. 7:7)
13. b (Gen. 7:2, 3)
14. d (Gen. 7:6)
15. d (Gen. 7:11)
16. a (Gen. 7:11, 8:14)
17. b (Gen. 8:6-10)
18. b (Gen. 8:8, 9)
19. d (Gen. 8:12)
20. a
21. e (Gen. 9:20-21)
22. d (Gen. 9:8-16)
23. b (It was Mt. Ararat, Not Mt. Sinai)

(Adapted from an idea contributed by Charles Wiltrout, New Labanon, Ohio)

Chapter Four

Special Events

BANANA NIGHT III

Here are some more banana games to go with those already listed for the "Banana Night" (*IDEAS Number Sixteen*) and "Banana Night II" (*IDEAS Number Nineteen*). The basic idea behind a Banana Night is to have everyone come dressed in banana colors (yellow, brown, or green) and then play all kinds of games that involve the use of bananas. Here are three more:

1. *Shoot Out At The O.K. Banana:* Get two people and stand them about ten feet apart (give them some "real" cowboy hats to wear for effect). Then give them their "irons"—which are bananas. They put them in their holsters (pockets) and on the word "draw" they pull their guns out, peel them and then eat them. The first one to completely swallow theirs is the winner.
2. *Banana Eating Contest:* Get a number of people situated around a table with their hands tied behind their backs. Then put an unpeeled banana (or two) in front of them. When you say "go" they must peel and eat their bananas without using their hands. Have some towels on hand as it gets real messy. The first to swallow their bananas is the winner. This one can also be done with couples. A couple gets an unpeeled banana, and together they must try to unpeel it without using their hands and eat the banana. It's a riot to watch.
3. *The P.B. Banfizz Race:* This is a variation of the game "Un-Banana" (*IDEAS Number One*) and involves peanut butter. Select your contestants and then cover their bananas with peanut butter (chunky is best). They will proceed on the word "go" to eat their banana and then polish it off with a glass of 7-up or Sprite. The combination usually creates a foamy mess in their mouths. The first to successfully eat their banana and drink their drink wins the race.

(Contributed by Carl Campbell, Huntington Valley, Pennsylvania)

HOUSE-TO-HOUSE PUZZLE HUNT

This is a "treasure hunt" with a new twist that really makes it different and fun. It requires a lot of preparation, but the results are well worth the effort. Here's how it works.

First, you will need to line up a number of homes (of church members) where the people are willing to stay home the night of this event and help out. The number of homes that you need will vary,

but you will probably need at least five or six. Eight or nine is ideal.

On the night of the event, you divide the group into car loads (each team traveling together), or you can do this event on bicycles or on (foot if) all the houses are within close walking distance. When the groups leave the starting point, they are each given one piece to a puzzle (a children's puzzle which has eight or nine pieces to it). On the back of the puzzle piece is the name of a family in the church. They must go to that family's house, where they will be given an instruction. They must then do whatever the instruction tells them to do, and they will be given another puzzle piece. This puzzle piece will tell them where they are to go next. At the next house, they do the same thing. The group that arrives back at the starting place with all their puzzle pieces, and successfully puts their puzzle together first, is the winner.

Obviously, the number of homes must be the same as the number of puzzle pieces you have. Each team should have a different route, so that everyone isn't going to the same house at the same time. You can also give each group a different puzzle, so long as the number of pieces is the same. This will involve some advance preparation in which you assign each group a number, and when they arrive at each house they receive the puzzle piece with the appropriate number on it. You can set it up so that each group is taking the houses in a different order.

At each house there is a different instruction which the group must do before they are given their puzzle piece. The instructions can be things like:

1. Tell three jokes to the family who lives at this house.
2. Form a pyramid and sing a Christmas carol while in that position.
3. Run three laps around the house.
4. Everyone chew a wad of bubble gum and blow a bubble together at the same time.
5. Together, recite John 3:16.
6. Eat a peanut butter and jelly sandwich (provided there) and have a glass of punch.

The last piece of the puzzle for each group should instruct them to head back to the starting location. Award prizes to the winners, serve refreshments, share experiences, and have a good time of fellowship. It's a lot of fun. (Contributed by Syd Schnaars, Delaware, Ohio)

MEMORIZATION TREASURE HUNT

A city park works the best for this hunt. Before the group arrives, you hide verses of Scripture around the park in various places, by taping them to objects, i.e., under a park bench, on the bottom of a swing seat, on the back of a sign, etc. Then you need to prepare riddle-

type clues, giving as little information about the locations as possible. ("Something mothers spend much time on," could be a clue for under a park bench.) The group is divided into small groups of 3 or 4 and each small group is given their first clue. They are then instructed to find the Scripture, memorize it, and come back and recite it, without removing it from the object. Upon successfully doing this, they receive their next clue. Everyone should receive the same clues but in a different order. The first group reciting the last verse wins the hunt. (Contributed by Kent Bloomquist, Albuquerque, New Mexico)

MISSING PARENT HUNT

Here's a great special event that involves both the kids and their parents. First, you will need to call a meeting for the parents of your youth. Explain that you would like to help them in relating to their teenagers, and that you have an activity that will help do that, and be a lot of fun at the same time. The parents' role in this activity is to disguise themselves in a way which will keep the kids in the youth group from recognizing them. Then, you pick the busiest place you can find in your area, like a large airport, or a big shopping mall where there are lots of people. The parents station themselves somewhere in the crowd. They must be in plain view, trying to be as inconspicuous as possible, but they cannot actually hide.

Once the parents are ready, the object is to see which young person can identify the most parents. Establish a time limit according to the number of parents you have. When a kid thinks he or she has found a parent, he must obtain the parent's signature. However, the young person must give the "password" in order for the parent to sign, which is "MOMMY, MOMMY!" or "DADDY, DADDY!" depending on the sex of the parent. After the time limit is up, everyone meets together for refreshments and awards to the kids finding the most parents. You can also give awards to the parents for the "Least Located Parent," "Best (or worst) Disguise," etc. It's a lot of fun. (Contributed by Rick McPeak, Greenville, Illinois)

A MUDDING

This is the kind of event most kids dream about. Find some land, get permission to dig it up, and then wet it down sufficiently to create a big area of good sloshy mud. You want an area big enough to play games in, and preferably with mud that is a foot or two deep. Then play the games described below, or any others that you can think of. Make sure the kids wear clothes that can be ruined for good. During the event have a couple of hoses on hand to keep the mud nice and gooey, and you can use them to wash off the kids when necessary. Some suggested mud games:

1. *Mud Packing:* Divide into teams and have them cover one

member of their team completely with mud (except for the head, of course). Judge for best job.

2. *Mud Sculptures:* See which team can create the most recognizable form out of the mud. This must be done within a specified time limit.

3. *Mud Ball:* Use your imagination here. The best ballgame to play is a variation of football, with tackling in the mud, etc. Any other ballgame can also be played.

4. *Mud Jumping:* Set up a track or ramp, and have kids jump for distance into the mud. Splat.

5. *Mud Drag Races:* The guys on each team lie down on their backs and the girls grab the feet of the guys and pull them across the mud hole and back, relay-fashion. This could be done with all the girls helping out, or two girls per guy, etc. Then reverse it, with the guys pulling the girls across through the mud. They love it.

6. *Mud Slinging:* Again, use your imagination for this. You could have any number of contests that involve throwing mud (at each other, at a target, etc.). Whoever wins can be given the award as the "Politician of the Day."

Finish up by hosing everyone off (you might even take the kids to a local car wash to get cleaned up). Don't forget to take movies. (Contributed by Larry Lawrence, Jonesboro, Georgia)

ODD BALL OLYMPICS

Here is another approach to an "Olympic-type" event featuring all kinds of wild and crazy games from the *IDEAS* Library. Have the kids divide into teams (countries) and compete against each other for the "gold medal." Here are some suggested events that you can use in addition to the dozens of others that you can find in *IDEAS:*

1. *The Balloon Hurl:* This is simply shot-putting with a big balloon. Draw a circle on the floor or ground which the hurler must stay in, and give him (or her) a balloon to shot-put for distance. This can really be unpredictable when done outside on a breezy day.

2. *Olympic Egg-Tossing:* Mark a line on the ground, and put markers on it at one or two yard intervals. Each team has two "tossers" who stand on the line two yards apart to begin with, and toss the raw egg back and forth once. They may then elect to step backwards one yard (on both sides) and toss again. If the egg breaks they lose half the distance they have gone so far. They may stop anytime they want after a successful toss, and their score is recorded.

3. *Iced-T Race:* Boys on each team wear T-shirts that are tucked in and tied around the waist with a belt or rope. A bucket of ice is dumped into the boys T-shirt (down the neck), and the boy must run around a goal and back. Several boys do this, each time carrying the same ice inside their shirts. The last boy dumps the

ice back into the bucket and the team that has the most ice still in their bucket wins.

4. *Balloon Juggling:* This one is best when done indoors. Each contestant stands in the middle of a big pile of blown-up balloons. On a signal, he or she must try to get as many balloons up in the air as possible, holding them up off the ground. When the time limit is up, count how many balloons are up. Give each person three tries and take the best score. (Contributed by Lawrence Stewart, Melrose, Iowa)

SAFARI

Here's an event that can make an ordinary trip to the zoo a lot more exciting. Divide the group into teams of roughly equal numbers. It doesn't matter how many teams there are. Each team is given a list of things to do or find inside the zoo and is given a time limit to complete the list. They do not have to do each assignment in order. It is best to place point values on each item and to encourage them to accumulate the highest number of points.

At the end of the time limit, gather together at some point within the zoo (most have picnic areas that would work great) and add up the points. They must be able to display any items that were to be brought back. The winning team members should all receive a prize—maybe something from the zoo's souvenir stand.

Some sample items that might be on the Safari list:

1. Make up a song about your youth pastor, an elephant, and a monkey (50 points)
2. Bring back some animal food (15) Fifty points if it is alive.
3. Who is Sam? (10) (*The name of an animal in the zoo.*)
4. Signature of a male zoo keeper. (15)
5. Lip-prints of a female zookeeper. (50)
6. What is the youngest animal in the zoo? (5)
7. What is the oldest animal in the zoo? (5)
8. What is an Oxyrinchus Pichanosis? (15)
9. Find the "Australian Grodfog" (50) (*A lady sitting on a bench near the kangaroos, dressed strangely and wearing a fake mustache.*)
10. Find the "Great Mau-Mau" (50) (*This can be two people in the zoo tied together with string each wearing a name tag saying "mau."*)
11. Walk through the Aviary singing "Bird drops keep falling on my head." (30)
12. Pet every animal in the petting zoo. (35)
13. Bring back a dead fish. (45)
14. Sing Happy Birthday to a Hippo (20)
15. Talk to a gorilla for five minutes without stopping. (40)

16. Find the smelliest animal in the zoo. (40)

(Contributed by Tim Jack, Sun Valley, California)

SPONSOR PAINTING

This crazy idea is best used at the beginning of the year when introducing new youth sponsors to the group, although it could take place anytime. The youth sponsors hide and the group divides into the same number of groups as there are sponsors. On a signal, each group holds hands and as a group tries to locate one of the sponsors. Once they find one, they bring him (or her) back to a central location, where there is a supply of watercolor paint and brushes. Each group then tries to outdo the other in painting designs all over their youth sponsor's body. Obviously, this idea must be used with some discretion, as some youth sponsors may not appreciate this idea as much as the kids. For female sponsors, you might want to restrict the painting to the face, arms and legs, for obvious reasons. The purpose, of course, is to have fun, and to introduce the sponsors to the group in a creative way. (Contributed by Ruth Staal, Grand Rapids, Michigan)